STECK-VAUGHN
CRITICAL THINKING

Reading, Thinking, and Reasoning Skills

Authors

Don Barnes
Professor of Education
Ball State University; Muncie, Indiana

Arlene Burgdorf
Former Resource Consultant
Hammond Indiana Public Schools

L. Stanley Wenck
Professor of Educational Psychology
Ball State University; Muncie, Indiana

Consultant

Gloria Sesso
Supervisor of Social Studies
Half Hollow Hills School District; Dix Hills, New York

LEVEL						
A	B	C	D	E	F

STECK-VAUGHN
COMPANY
ELEMENTARY • SECONDARY • ADULT • LIBRARY

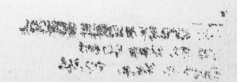

ACKNOWLEDGMENTS

Executive Editor
Elizabeth Strauss

Project Editor
Anita Arndt

Consulting Editor
Melinda Veatch

Design, Production, and Editorial Services
The Quarasan Group, Inc.

Contributing Writers
Tara McCarthy
Linda Ward Beech

Cover Design
Linda Adkins Graphic Design

Photography:
p. 5   — H. Armstrong Roberts
p. 29   — Nita Winter
p. 53   — Nita Winter
p. 75   — Nita Winter

Illustration:
pp. 6, 19, 72, 85 — Ruth Brunke
pp. 7, 59 — Nancy Walter
pp. 8, 18, 21, 25, 34, 42, 48, 61, 77, 94 — Dave Blanchette
pp. 9, 13, 16, 23, 26, 27, 28, 32, 35, 38, 43, 49, 51, 52, 68, 75, 78, 92, 95, 96 — Kenneth Smith
pp. 11, 14, 17, 24, 30, 33, 36, 41, 46, 50, 63, 66, 69, 70, 76, 79, 86, 90, 93 — Lynn McClain
pp. 12, 15, 20, 54, 58, 60, 62, 64, 74, 80, 87, 89, 96 — Scott Bieser
pp. 31, 37 — Peg Dougherty
pp. 57, 65, 67, 71, 91 — Elizabeth Allen

ISBN 0–8114–6600–0

TABLE OF CONTENTS

TABLE OF CONTENTS

Knowing

Knowing means getting the facts together. Let's try it out. How many children are in the picture? What are they doing? Do you know why one boy is doing something different?

5

Put an **X** on each animal that does not belong on a farm.

Name

6

Circle the things that belong in a tool box.

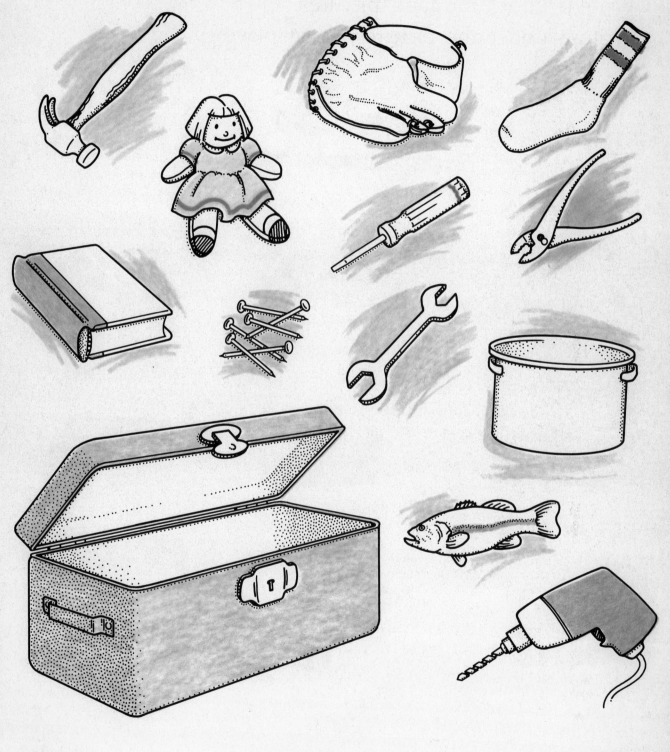

Name _____

Write **1** under the animal pictures.

Write **2** under the food pictures.

Write **3** under the pictures about playing.

Name

Write the word that tells where you wear each thing.

hands	feet	head	body

_____   _____   _____

_____   _____   _____

_____   _____   _____

_____   _____   _____

Name _____

Write each word in the drawing where it belongs.

Sue
hat
zoo
egg
boy
store
girl
home
ring
pen
Sam
city

People

Places

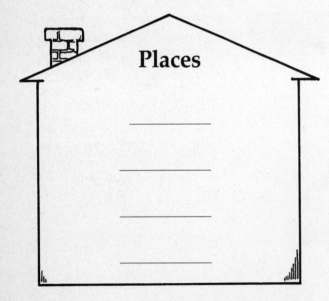

Things

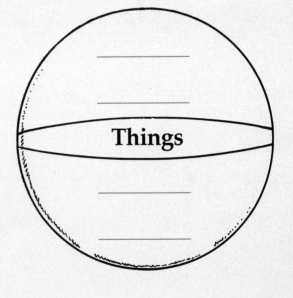

Name

Circle the pictures of make-believe animals.

Name

Write **R** if the thing is real.
Write **M** if the thing is make-believe.

___

___

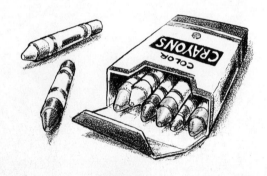

___

___

___

___

___

___

Name _____

Circle the picture that makes the sentence make-believe.

1. Sara and Jim rode on a

2. The fence was painted by a

3. We climbed a tree and picked

4. In the grass, I stepped on an

5. Dan and Fran slid down the

Name _____

Circle the picture that makes the sentence tell about something real.

1. Joe and Mary found a

2. The car was driven by a

3. Mom and I planted

4. We jumped on a

5. I rode on a

Name

Critical Thinking, Level A © 1993 Steck-Vaughn

Write **fact** after each sentence that tells a fact.

1. The dress has three buttons. _____

   I think dresses are nice. _____

2. We think the doll is funny. _____

   The doll has white socks. _____

3. I think dogs are cute. _____

   The dog has spots. _____

4. I think the dog is big. _____

   The dog has a tail. _____

5. I think the dress is clean. _____

   The dress has long sleeves. _____

Name _____

Write **O** before each sentence that tells an opinion.

1. ____ A ball is round.

   ____ Balls go too fast.

2. ____ A boat ride is not fun.

   ____ A boat floats on water.

3. ____ An apple is a kind of fruit.

   ____ I think apples are too sweet.

4. ____ Plants are very pretty.

   ____ Plants live and grow.

5. ____ Clocks are better than watches.

   ____ Clocks and watches tell time.

Name _____

Critical Thinking, Level A © 1993 Steck-Vaughn

Write **F** if the sentence tells a fact.

Write **O** if the sentence tells an opinion.

Peanuts are too salty.

Acorns are nuts.

Some nuts grow on trees.

_____

Airplanes are fun.

Planes land at airports.

Some planes are small.

_____

Brick houses are best.

My house is pretty.

Houses can be made of wood.

_____

Name _____

17

Read each story. Find the sentence that tells an opinion. Copy that sentence on the line.

1. I think camping is fun. We hike to the lake. We carry our tent and some food. We bring a camera and some books.

_____

2. Jill will be in a play. She will be the princess. Jill's mother made her a new dress. Jill thinks the dress is beautiful. She will wear it in the play.

_____

Name _____

Critical Thinking, Level A © 1993 Steck-Vaughn

Read the word under each picture.
Write the word under the correct definition.

whale   **butterfly**   **kangaroo**

bee   **shark**   **rabbit**

1. Animals that fly

   _____   _____

2. Animals that swim

   _____   _____

3. Animals that hop

   _____   _____

Name _____

A. Write a word from the **Word Box** to begin each sentence.

Word Box

Toys
Chairs
Boats
Fruit

1. ———— grows on trees.

2. ———— go on the water.

3. ———— are things you play with.

4. ———— are things to sit on.

B. Write the correct number by each picture.

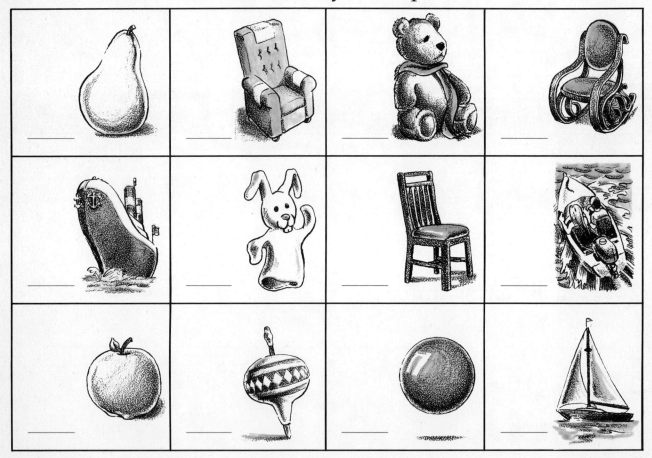

Name _____

Critical Thinking, Level A © 1993 Steck-Vaughn

20

A. Draw a line from each word to the sentence that tells about it.

Clothes   You plant them.   _____ _____

Animals   You wear them.   _____ _____

Flowers   They live in the
                 woods.   _____ _____

B. Write each word after the sentence it goes with.

deer   roses   shoes

mums   bears   hats

Name

A. Read the word in each box. Draw a picture to show what the word means.

1. food	2. book

3. bed	4. kitten

B. Write each sentence under the picture it goes with.

This is something to read.

This is a pet.

This is something to sleep in.

This is something to eat.

Name _____

Critical Thinking, Level A © 1993 Steck-Vaughn

Draw a line from each picture to the sentence that tells about it.

Use your hands.   Use your feet.

Name _____

Write the letter of each picture on the line where it belongs.

A.

1. Animals

——— walk.

——— climb.

——— eat.

——— sleep.

2. Children

——— climb.

——— slide.

——— walk.

B.

E.

C.

F.

D.

G.

Name _____

Where does each thing belong? Write its letter on a line next to the picture of the place.

circus

barn

store

Name

25

A. Read the story.

The Tiger Cubs

Not many tiger cubs are born at the zoo. But this year three of them were born.

One was fat and liked to sleep. Another was playful. Another looked a little sad.

Soon, the cubs began to grow. They did not want to stay in their playpen.

Their keeper had fun with them. They were just like big kittens.

B. Write the word that belongs in each blank.

The tiger cubs were born at the _____.

jungle playpen zoo

There were _____ tiger cubs. They

two three four

stayed in a _____. The tiger cubs

yard cage playpen

were just like big _____.

kittens lions bears

Name _____

A. Classifying

Color the two toys blue.
Color the real animals brown.
Color the fruit yellow.

B. Definition and Example

Read each word group. Look
at the picture. Find something
that the word group tells about. Write the word.

1. a kind of toy _____

2. something to eat _____

3. a thing that is alive _____

C. Real and Make-Believe

Choose one thing that is shown in the picture.
Write about something make-believe that it could do.

_____

_____

_____

Name _____

D. Fact and Opinion

Study the pictures at the bottom of the page. Then finish each sentence in your own way.

1. The most beautiful animal is the _____.

2. The smallest animal is the _____.

3. The best pet would be the _____.

4. The animal with the long neck is an _____.

E. Outlining and Summarizing

Read the sentences you finished. Write the number of each sentence under the correct heading below.

Fact	Opinion
_____	_____
_____	_____

elephant   monkey   ostrich

Name _____

Understanding

Understanding means telling about something in your own words. What's happening in the picture? Where did the bubbles come from? Can the boy make more bubbles? How?

Comparing and Contrasting

In each row, put an **X** on the thing that is different.

1.

2.   pay   play   play

3.

4.

5.

6.

7.

8.

Name

Critical Thinking, Level A © 1993 Steck-Vaughn

Circle the things that get shorter after they are used.

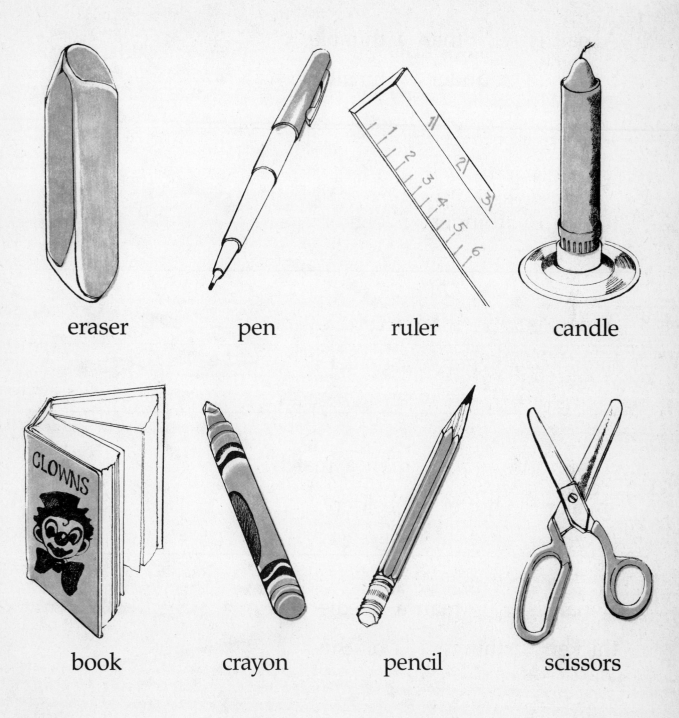

eraser   pen   ruler   candle

book   crayon   pencil   scissors

Name

Circle the word that makes the sentence tell about the pictures.

1. A pail is ____ than a thimble.
   bigger   rounder   smaller

_____

2. A pencil is ____ than a log.
   thicker   thinner   bigger

_____

3. A pan is ____ than a tub.
   higher   bigger   smaller

_____

4. A campfire is ____ than a match.
   smaller   hotter   colder

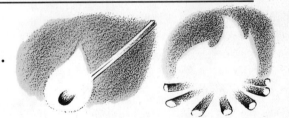

_____

5. A nail is ____ than a needle.
   thicker   thinner   brighter

Name _____

Draw a line from the picture of each part to the object it belongs to.

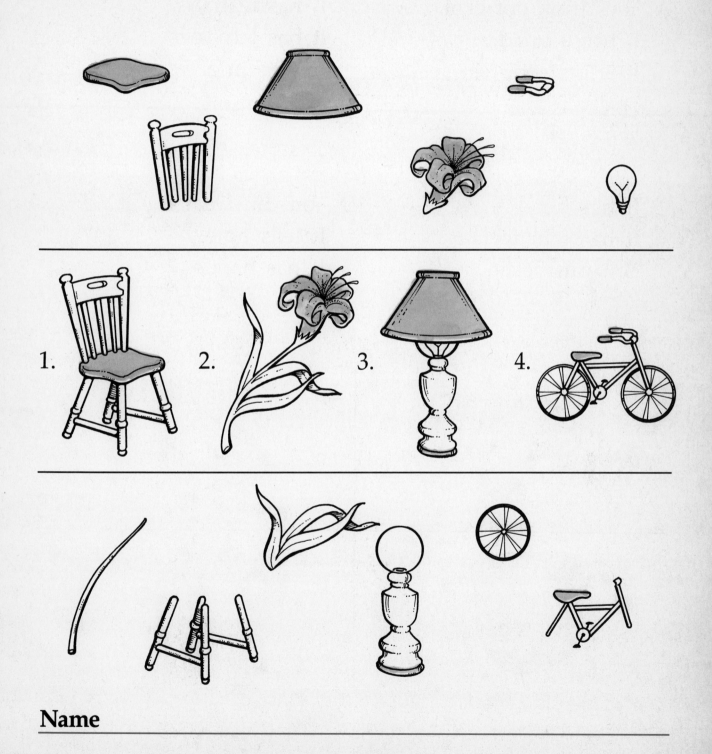

1.   2.   3.   4.

Name

Write the number of the picture the riddle tells about.

A. You drink out of it.
It has a handle.
It is part of a set
of dishes.

_____

B. It has feathers.
It has two legs.
It lives in a tree.

_____

C. It has fur.
It has four feet.
You can pet it.

_____

D. You can wear it.
It tells time.
It has hands.

_____

1.

2.

3.

4.

Name _____

Number the pictures in order to show how to make a paper bag mask.

Name

Steps in a Process

Number the pictures of the animals to show the order in which Clara sees them.

Name _____

Critical Thinking, Level A © 1993 Steck-Vaughn

In each row, number each picture **1**, **2**, or **3** to show what happened first, second, and last.

A.

_____   _____   _____

B.

_____   _____   _____

C.

_____   _____   _____

D.

_____   _____   _____

Name _____

Number each picture to show the order of how a flower grows.

Name

Critical Thinking, Level A © 1993 Steck-Vaughn

A. Color each shape. Use the color named below it.

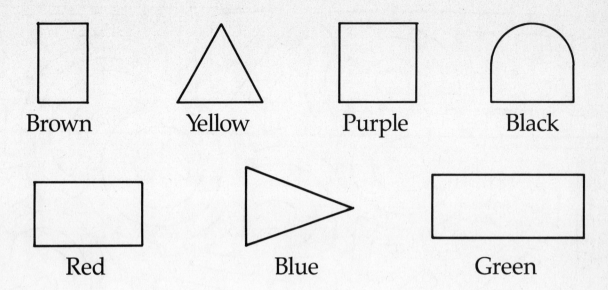

Brown   Yellow   Purple   Black

Red   Blue   Green

B. Now color the picture. Color each shape the same color as above.

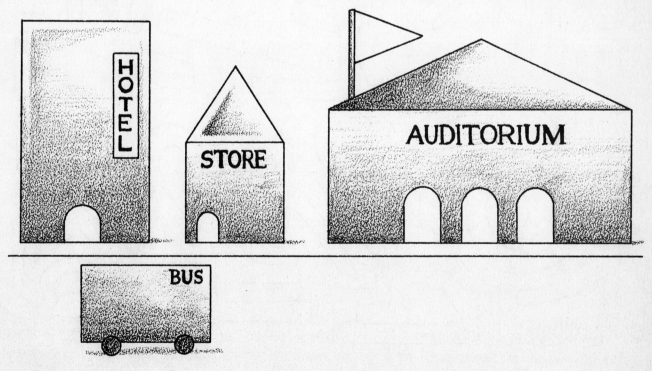

Name

Color the 6 numerals hidden in the picture.

Name _____

Critical Thinking, Level A © 1993 Steck-Vaughn

Circle the word that means about the same as the numbered word.

small   =   little

                glad

1. happy   many

                paint

2. pick   choose

                large

3. big   back

                then

4. thin   slim

                quick

5. fast   cold

                said

6. see   look

                below

7. under   walk

Name

41

Write the opposite of each numbered word.

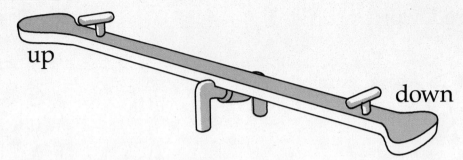

up   down

A. | wet   out   stop   far

1. go _____   2. dry _____

3. near _____   4. in _____

B. | on   sad   long   all

1. short _____   2. none _____

3. off _____   4. happy _____

C. | over   yes   give   weak

1. take _____   2. strong _____

3. no _____   4. under _____

Name _____

Critical Thinking, Level A © 1993 Steck-Vaughn

Circle the sentence that tells the main idea of each picture.

A.

1. Do you like to play?
2. Mary, Jan, and Lee are friends.
3. We jump rope.

B.

1. I like to draw pictures.
2. The school had an art fair.
3. Art is fun.

C.

1. Our team won the game.
2. Baseball is a sport.
3. We play together.

D.

1. Clowns are funny.
2. I like the circus.
3. Lions and tigers are in a circus.

Name _____

43

Circle the best name for each story.

A. We went to the store.
We went to get a toy.
The toy is for Marco.
Marco will like this toy.

1. The Store
2. A Toy for Marco
3. The Pet Store

B. Jill has a surprise.
It is in a box.
It is a little hat.
The hat is for Patty.

1. A Little Box
2. A New Dress
3. A Hat for Patty

C. Mother sees something.
It is white.
It has red ribbons.
It is a surprise for
Mother.

1. A Hat
2. A Red Apple
3. A Gift for Mother

D. The children are at a
party.
They put on funny hats.
They are happy.
They play games.

1. A Cake
2. A Birthday Party
3. Funny Hats

Name

Critical Thinking, Level A © 1993 Steck-Vaughn

Circle the sentence that tells the main idea of each story.

1. It is a school day. Some children are reading. We are doing math. We are all busy.

2. We are going to give a play. Some children will learn lines. Some will help paint. We will all sing.

3. We will go to the zoo today. I want to see the bears. We will see other animals, too.

4. We like to jump rope. Lisa and Jan hold the rope. John jumps. Lee waits in line.

5. The circus will be here soon. We will see a parade. We will see clowns. Animals will do tricks.

6. Jeff has a new bicycle. It has a horn. It has a light. Jeff rides it each day.

Name

Write the sentence that tells the main idea.

1.   The mouse ran under the table. The mouse ran to the kitchen. A cat was chasing the mouse.

_____

_____

2.   The farmer fed the hen and chicks. The hen pecked at the yellow food. The chicks pecked the ground.

_____

_____

3.   Joan is my sister. Tod and Ted are my brothers. I have a big family.

_____

_____

Name

Choose a word from the **Color Key** to finish each sentence.

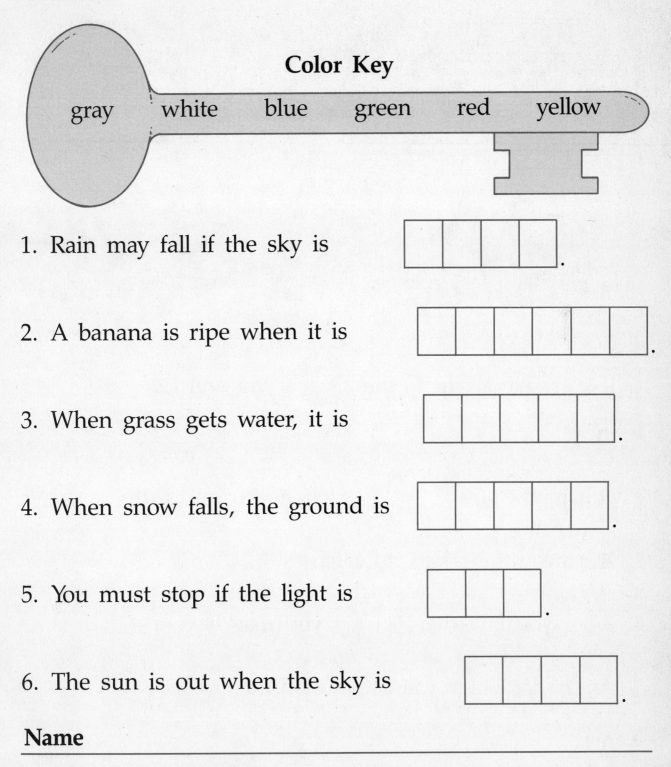

Color Key

gray   white   blue   green   red   yellow

1. Rain may fall if the sky is ⬜⬜⬜⬜.

2. A banana is ripe when it is ⬜⬜⬜⬜⬜⬜.

3. When grass gets water, it is ⬜⬜⬜⬜⬜.

4. When snow falls, the ground is ⬜⬜⬜⬜⬜.

5. You must stop if the light is ⬜⬜⬜.

6. The sun is out when the sky is ⬜⬜⬜⬜.

Name

Write the letter of the picture that will finish each sentence.

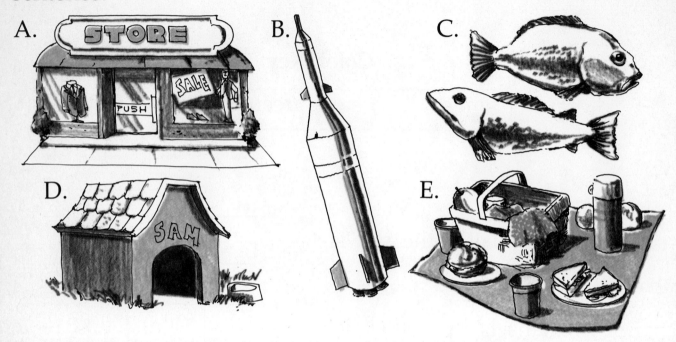

A.   B.   C.

D.   E.

1. If you take a trip to the 🌙 , you will ride

in a ____.

2. You might buy a 👕 when you go to the ____.

3. You need a 🎣 to catch ____.

4. After you buy the 🍎🧃 , you may have a ____.

5. A 🐕 may want to sleep in a ____.

Name

Critical Thinking, Level A © 1993 Steck-Vaughn

Circle the word that best fits into each sentence.

1. A window is part of a room, which is part of a

   floor.   room.   building.

2. Shep is the name of a dog, which is a kind of

   animal.   baby.   toy.

3. A leaf is part of a tree, which is one kind of

   tree.   plant.   fruit.

4. Lettuce is part of a salad, which is a kind of

   toy.   cake.   food.

5. A tire is part of a wheel, which is part of a

   tool.   boat.   car.

Name _____

Identifying Relationships

Write the letter of the picture that shows what is needed for the sentence to make sense.

A. B. C.

D. E. F.

1. Because there is no wind, the kite is like picture _____.

2. If the wind blows, the kite will be like picture _____.

3. If the sun shines, Mary will play outside, as in

   picture _____.

4. If May wants to go outside, she will be at the door, as

   in picture _____.

5. To stay cool, you will need _____.

6. To have leaves, you must first have _____.

Name

A. Identifying Main Ideas
   Comparing and Contrasting
   Identifying Structure

Look at the picture. Then answer the questions.

1. What are the children doing? _____

2. Which building is smallest? _____

3. Which building needs more work? _____

B. Steps in a Process

Look at the picture again. Tell how you could help.

_____

_____

Name _____

51

C. Understanding Pictures
Comparing Word Meanings

Look at the picture. Then answer the questions.

1. Which animals are on the bench? _____

_____

2. Which animal is under the bench? _____

3. Which animal is beside the bench? _____

4. Which animal is smallest? _____

D. Identifying Relationships

Finish each sentence.

1. If you want a pet that can purr, get a _____

2. If you want a pet that can fly, get a _____

Name _____

Critical Thinking, Level A © 1993 Steck-Vaughn

Applying

Applying means using what you know. Look at the picture. How are the children dressed? What are they doing? Do you think it is a special dance? Why or why not?

A. Put **1** beside the smallest. Put **3** beside the largest.
   Put **2** beside the other one.

_____   _____   _____

B. Put **1** beside the slowest. Put **3** beside the fastest.
   Put **2** beside the other one.

_____   _____   _____

C. Put **1** beside the shortest. Put **3** beside the tallest.
   Put **2** beside the other one.

_____

Name

Write one letter to make a word in each body part.
Begin with **a.** Continue in alphabetical order.

a b c d e f g h i j k l m n o p q r s t u v w x y z

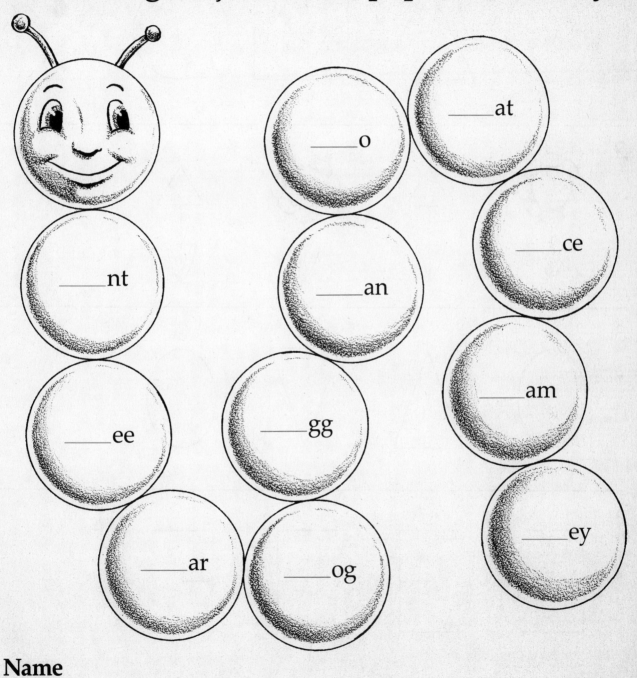

_____o

_____at

_____nt

_____an

_____ce

_____ee

_____gg

_____am

_____ar

_____og

_____ey

Name

Draw the next object in each row.

1.

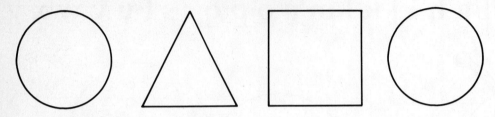

2.

 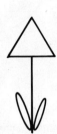  

3.

4.

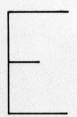   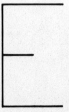

Name

Critical Thinking, Level A © 1993 Steck-Vaughn

Write **yes** if the objects shown on the right will fit what is in the box. Write **no** if they will not fit.

_____ 1.

_____ 2.

_____ 3.

_____ 4.

_____ 5.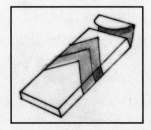

Name _____

Circle the picture of each thing that is small enough to fit inside Don's lunch box.

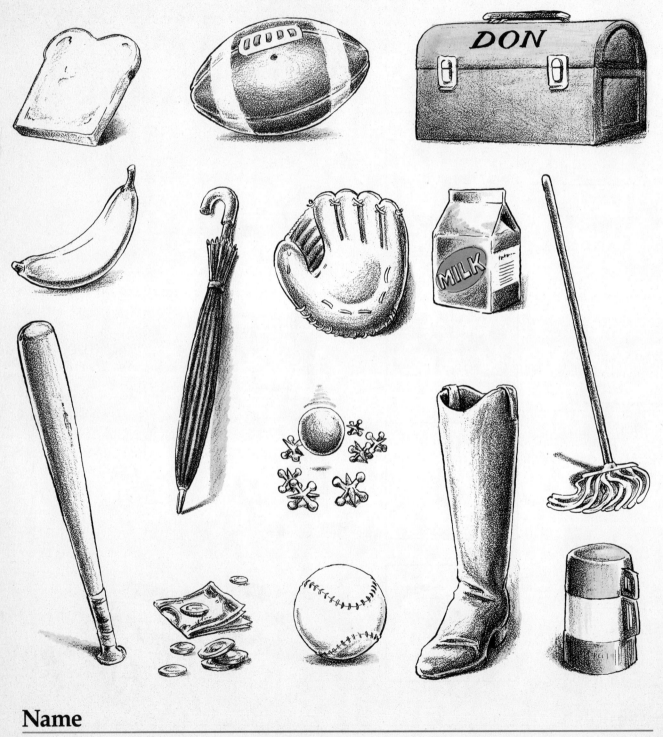

Name

Look at each object in the box. Circle the picture in the row that is the right size for it.

1.

2.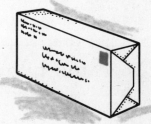

3.

4.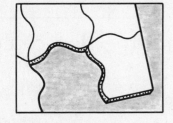

5.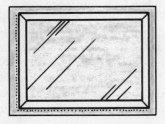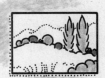

Name

A. Circle the number of the bowl that the fish could swim in.

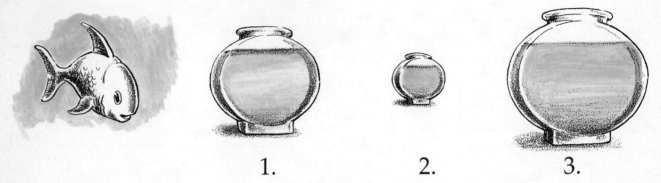

1.   2.   3.

B. Circle the number of the box that will fit under the bed.

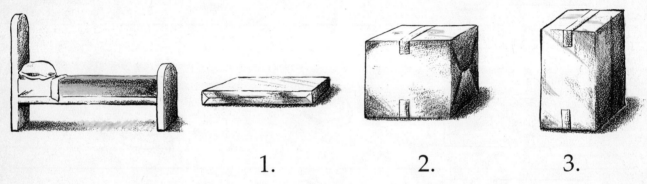

1.   2.   3.

C. Circle the number of the doghouse that the dog could live in.

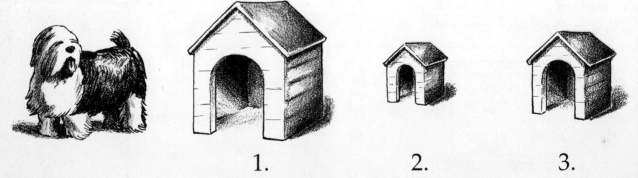

1.   2.   3.

Name

Critical Thinking, Level A © 1993 Steck-Vaughn

Draw a line from each numbered picture to the picture that shows what will probably happen next.

1.

2.

3.

4.

Name _____

Thinking About What Will Happen

A. Draw lines to tell what will happen to each object if it is left in the sun.

melt

stay the same

B. Draw lines to tell what will happen to each object if it is put into water.

get soft

stay the same

Name

Thinking About What Will Happen

Draw a picture to show what will probably happen next in each row.

A.

B.

C.

Name _____

Circle the right ending for each sentence.

1. If you put water on a fire, it would
   A. go out.
   B. burn.

2. If you put meat on a hot stove, it would
   A. get cold.
   B. cook.

3. If you put ice in sunlight, it would
   A. melt.
   B. freeze.

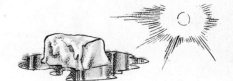

4. If you put sand in your hair, your hair would be
   A. clean.
   B. dirty.

5. If you put water on a plant, it would
   A. grow.
   B. die.

6. If you put water on a piece of paper, it would
   A. get wet.
   B. grow.

Name

Critical Thinking, Level A © 1993 Steck-Vaughn

Look at each picture. Put an **X** if you can be sure the sentence for each picture is true.

1. _____ It is cloudy outside.

2. _____ This lunch box belongs to Mike Fox.

3. _____ The turtle will win.

4. _____ This is Katy's dog.

5. _____ It is a fall day.

Name _____

Draw a line from each story to the picture that shows why something happened in the story.

1. Fred pulled the sheet under his chin. He did not come when we called him.

2. Suzie ran into the house. "I need a bandage," she said.

3. Fred was at the lake. He played by the water. All of a sudden, he was dripping wet.

4. Fred got out his jacket. He put on his boots. He took his umbrella outside.

5. Suzie looked down at the clouds. The houses looked tiny as she went past them.

Name

Look at the first picture in each row. Circle the picture that explains why the child feels that way.

1.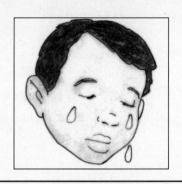

2.

3.

4.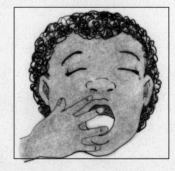

Name

Under each picture, write the number of the sentence that tells about it.

_____   _____   _____   _____

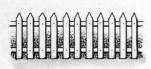   

_____   _____   _____   _____

1. Johnny was in trouble because he ate part of his mother's party food.

2. It swims and is sometimes a pet.

3. It might keep the dog from running away.

4. Children play with these toys.

5. It is round and you can wear it.

6. It could pinch you.

7. You use it at night.

8. It can wag its tail and bark.

Name

Write the word that sounds better in the sentence.

1. I will _____ over your checker and win the game. (take, jump)

2. The doctor said to _____ a glass of water. (take, drink)

3. Dad is going to _____ the new job. (take, carry)

4. Did you _____ time to wash your face? (take, use)

5. The bus will _____ you to school. (grab, take)

6. I will _____ my best shoes to the party. (take, wear)

7. Did you _____ your vitamins? (carry, take)

8. It is hard to _____ this heavy box. (carry, take)

9. She is going to _____ art lessons. (take, bring)

10. This dry plant _____ water. (needs, takes)

Name _____

A. Circle the picture that shows what each group of words means.

1. run into a friend

2. wake up on time

B. Draw pictures to show what the sentences mean.

1. Keep an eye on the dog.

2. Please give me a hand.

Name _____

Critical Thinking, Level A © 1993 Steck-Vaughn

A. Ordering Objects

Show the correct order by writing **1, 2,** and **3.**

1.

_____   _____   _____

2.

_____   _____   _____

B. Thinking About What Will Happen

What do you think will happen next to the girl above?
Put an **X** by the correct sentence.

_____ She will open the present herself.

_____ She will take the present to a party.

Name _____

C. Estimating

Circle the things that can be added to the shelf.

D. Inferring

Where is the shelf shown above? Put an **X** by the answer.

_____ in a bedroom   _____ in a kitchen

E. Changes in Word Meanings

Circle the picture that shows what each underlined word means.

1. My <u>pen</u> is out of ink.   a.    b.

2. Chris paid the <u>bill</u>.   a.    b.

3. Pat has the <u>bat</u> and ball.   a.   b.

Name _____

Critical Thinking, Level A © 1993 Steck-Vaughn

Analyzing

Analyzing means seeing how parts fit together. Look at the picture. What is the girl doing? What do you think she is listening to? How do you know?

Finish drawing each picture.

Name

Finish drawing the clown.

Name

Complete each sentence by drawing a line from each sentence beginning to its ending.

Here is a clock   that has a wheel missing.

Here is a wagon   with pretty flowers on it.

Here is a ball   that is old and tall.

Here is a glass   with stars and stripes.

Name

Write **1**, **2**, or **3** under each picture to show which book tells about it.

Birds   Things to Make   Games

1.   2.   3.

Name _____

Write the letters of the pictures that best complete each sentence.

1. To reach a high shelf, you could use a ____ or a ____.

A

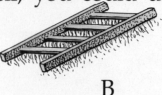
B

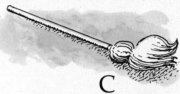
C

2. To go across a lake, you could use a ____ or a ____.

A

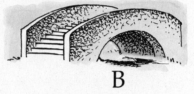
B

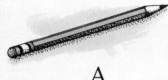
C

3. To draw a picture, you could use a ____ or a ____.

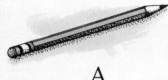
A

B

C

4. To see in the dark, you could use a ____ or a ____.

A

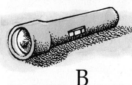
B

C

5. To clean up spilled milk, you could use a ____ or a ____.

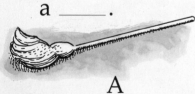
A

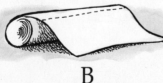
B

C

Name

Choose a word from the box to complete each sentence.

fly	heaters	sounds	covers

1. A  rings. A sings.

   They both make _____.

2. A goes on a house. A goes on a bed.

   They both are _____.

3. A cooks food. The  makes you warm.

   They both are _____.

4. A has wings. A  has wings.

   They both _____.

Name _____

A. Write the number of letters in each word on the line after the word.

_____ house _____   _____ pink _____

_____ two _____   _____ yellow _____

Put **1** on the blank before the word with the smallest number of letters. Use **2** for the next word. Number the remaining words.

B. Use the words above to complete the story.

May lives in a big _ _ _ _ _. It has three bedrooms.

May's room has _ _ _ windows. Her room has

_ _ _ _ _ and _ _ _ _ _ _ paper.

May likes her room.

Name

Critical Thinking, Level A © 1993 Steck-Vaughn

A. Draw pictures of what you use to see, to hear, and to touch.

See	Hear	Touch

B. Circle each word that names something you can see, hear, or touch.

dog	guess	ball
happiness	song	apple
tree	spoon	idea
thought	birthday	love
sunset	fear	chair
color	table	toys
cup	air	box
hate	milk	bed

Name

Abstract or Concrete

Follow the numbers. Draw a line to connect each word that names something you can smell, taste, or see.

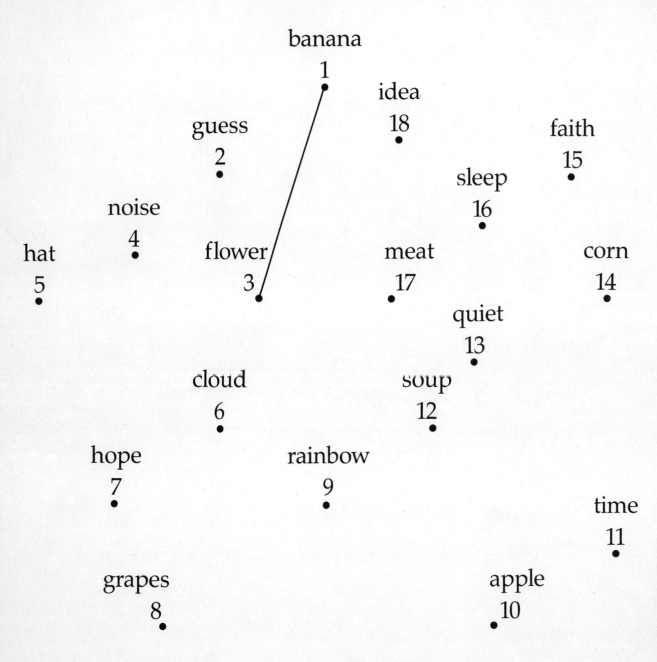

Name _____

Critical Thinking, Level A © 1993 Steck-Vaughn

Circle the words that name something you cannot draw easily. Try to draw a picture of each word you circled.

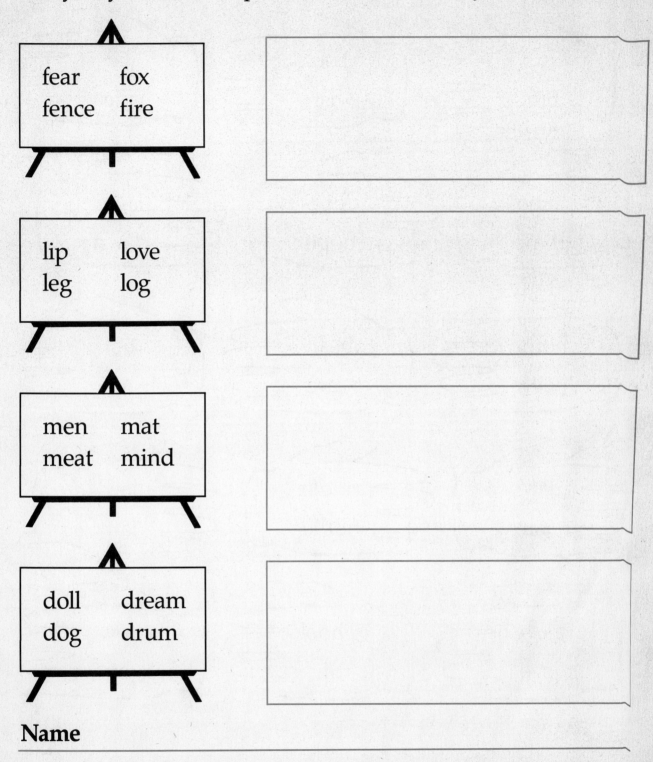

fear	fox
fence	fire

lip	love
leg	log

men	mat
meat	mind

doll	dream
dog	drum

Name

Abstract or Concrete

On each hand, cross out the word that names something you cannot touch.

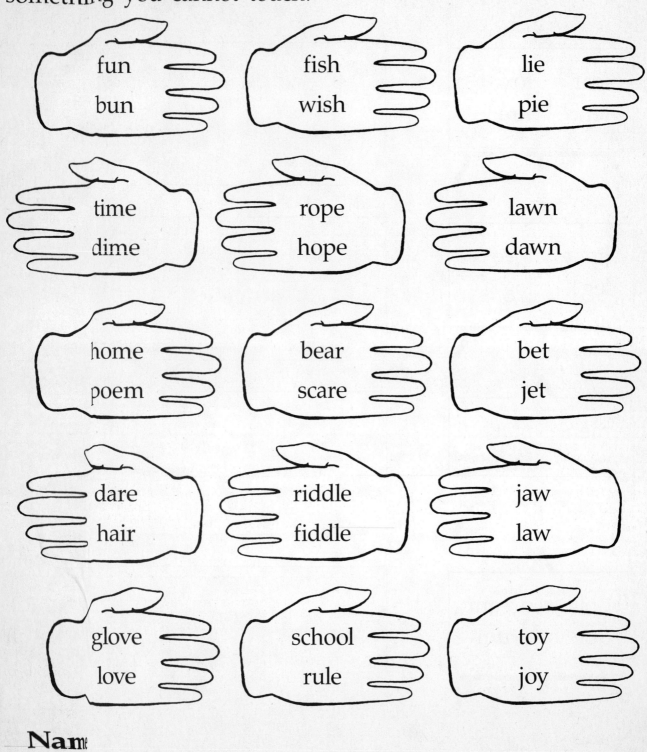

fun / bun	fish / wish	lie / pie
time / dime	rope / hope	lawn / dawn
home / poem	bear / scare	bet / jet
dare / hair	riddle / fiddle	jaw / law
glove / love	school / rule	toy / joy

Name

Write the letters that show what someone could make using the things shown in each box.

a.

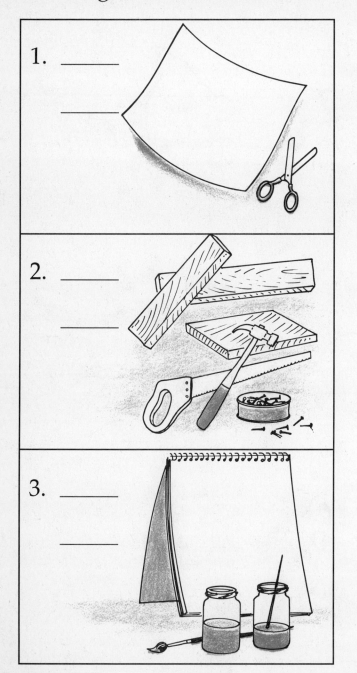

1. _____
   _____

2. _____
   _____

3. _____
   _____

b.

c.

d.

e.

f.

Name

Write the number of the place where each of the animals would live.

1. water

2. garden

3. tree

4. farm

5. house

6. woods

_____   _____

_____   _____

_____   _____

Name _____

Critical Thinking, Level A © 1993 Steck-Vaughn

Write the names of the things you would take on an overnight visit.

comb   toothbrush   bed

teddy bear   pajamas   lamp

piggy bank   cup   shoes

_____   _____   _____

_____   _____   _____

_____   _____   _____

Name _____

Put an **X** on the wrong word in each story. Circle the right word in the list below each story.

1.   Jean had a flat tire on her bike. She wanted to fix it, so she used a hammer.

nail   pump   knife

2.   Carlos went to the circus and saw the clowns. They were so merry, Carlos cried.

laughed   slept   jumped

3.   Sue had a very busy day. She went shopping. She was so tired she danced.

hopped   rested   ate

4.   Rudy had a round red balloon. He blew it up so far it popped. Now it is no longer red.

soft   flat   round

5.   Ming was walking to school. When he came to a red light he ran.

shouted   stopped   ate

6.   Betty had a birthday party. She got many nice presents. She was sad.

angry   mad   happy

Name _____

Critical Thinking, Level A © 1993 Steck-Vaughn

Write a rhyming word on each line.

1. The duck was put in a **sack.**

   And all it did was _____.

2. Jane will bounce the **ball,**

   When Judy gives her a _____.

3. My hands were so very **hot.**

   On my paper they left a _____.

4. A giraffe has a head so **high,**

   That it almost reaches the _____.

5. My pencil is so very **small.**

   I can't write with it at _____.

6. My garden will not **grow,**

   If I don't use the _____.

7. I worked very hard **today.**

   So now I can go and _____.

8. My dog is white and **black,**

   With spots upon its _____.

spot
play
hoe
all
quack
back
sky
call

Name

Read the story. Then circle the answer to each question.

Mother Bear has two cubs named Rin and Din. They have found a honey tree.

Poor Rin has just been stung by a bee. Din runs away quickly.

The honey tastes good, and the bears lie down to sleep. When they wake up, Rin and Din have fun playing.

1. Which animals did we meet in the story?
   A. Mother Bear, Rin, and Din
   B. Father Bear, Rin, and Din

2. Where are they?
   A. in the city
   B. in the woods

3. Why did they go to the tree?
   A. to climb
   B. to get honey

4. How did the honey taste?
   A. good
   B. bad

Name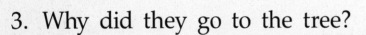

Critical Thinking, Level A © 1993 Steck-Vaughn

Put an X on the picture that does not belong. Write **1** and **2** to show the order in which things happen.

1. Making Soup

_____   _____   _____

2. Sending a Letter

_____   _____   _____

3. Making a Sand Castle

_____   _____   _____

Name _____

Draw a line under the sentence that you would take out or change.

1. My pencil is long.
    It is good to eat.
    I use it to write.

2. It is dark out.
    We will go to bed.
    It is time to play.

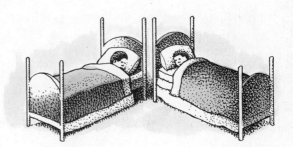

3. This is a house. It is
    a house for my dog.
    It is a very big house.

4. This is a nest. The
    birds live in the nest.
    The worm lives in the nest.

Name

Draw a line under the sentence that you would take out or change.

1. Today we had a fire drill.
    Everyone went outside.
    A king came to the drill.
    The firefighter told us
    that we did very well.

2. Tom has a new toy.
    It goes up into the air.
    You hold it by a handle.
    It has a tail, too.
    Did you guess that it is a kite?

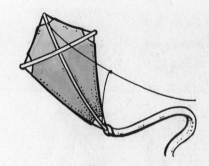

3. Soon it will be spring.
    There will be green grass.
    The flowers will come up.
    Snowflakes will come down.
    The days will be warm.

4. We went on a picnic.
    Mom made sandwiches.
    Dad brought the vacuum cleaner.
    I made lemonade.

Name

Number the pictures in the order in which they happened in the story.

Helen and the Horse

Helen would like to know how to ride a horse.
She gets on. Away she goes! Riding is not easy.
Helen does not learn to ride the first time she tries.

___

___

Name

A. **Judging Completeness**

Circle the things in the picture that are not complete.

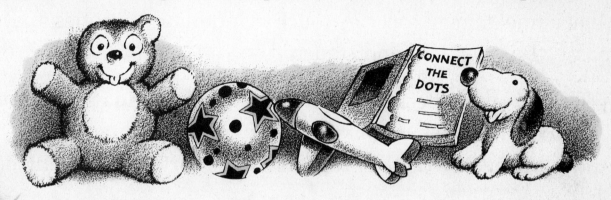

B. **Thinking About Facts That Fit**
Logic of Actions

Read the story. Cross out the sentence that does not belong.

Mary sorted her toys. She was going to fix them. She put her broken toys in one pile. Mary's dog was sleeping near the toys. She put her other toys in a different pile.

Circle the words that name things Mary could use to fix her broken toys.

water	glue	scissors
paper	wing	table
ear	milk	crayons

Name

C. Abstract or Concrete

Read the story. Look at the dark words. Circle the ones that name things you can touch. Underline the ones that name things you cannot touch.

Today was a special **day**. It was Juan's **birthday**. His **wish** was to have a **pet**. He liked colorful **fish**, talking **parrots**, and all **kinds** of cats. What would his birthday **present** be?

D. Parts of a Story
Story Logic

Circle the word that completes each sentence. The sentences tell a story, but they are not in order. Put a **1** before the sentence that happens first, a **2** before the sentence that happens next, and a **3** before the sentence that happens last.

_____ 1. The furry animal was a cat.
dog.

_____ 2. Dad brought home a big hat.
box.

_____ 3. A furry animal rock was in the box.

Name _____

Critical Thinking, Level A © 1993 Steck-Vaughn